S. HRG. 113–448

ANIMAL DRUG USER FEE AGREEMENTS: ADVANCING ANIMAL HEALTH FOR THE PUBLIC

HEARING

OF THE

COMMITTEE ON HEALTH, EDUCATION, LABOR, AND PENSIONS

UNITED STATES SENATE

ONE HUNDRED THIRTEENTH CONGRESS

FIRST SESSION

ON

EXAMINING ANIMAL DRUG USER FEE AGREEMENTS, FOCUSING ON ADVANCING ANIMAL HEALTH FOR THE PUBLIC HEALTH

FEBRUARY 27, 2013

Printed for the use of the Committee on Health, Education, Labor, and Pensions

Available via the World Wide Web: http://www.gpo.gov/fdsys/

U.S. GOVERNMENT PRINTING OFFICE

79–791 PDF   WASHINGTON : 2014

For sale by the Superintendent of Documents, U.S. Government Printing Office
Internet: bookstore.gpo.gov   Phone: toll free (866) 512–1800; DC area (202) 512–1800
Fax: (202) 512–2250   Mail: Stop SSOP, Washington, DC 20402–0001

(II)

C O N T E N T S

***

STATEMENTS

WEDNESDAY, FEBRUARY 27, 2013

Page

(III)

ANIMAL DRUG USER FEE AGREEMENTS: ADVANCING ANIMAL HEALTH FOR THE PUBLIC

WEDNESDAY, FEBRUARY 27, 2013

U.S. SENATE,
COMMITTEE ON HEALTH, EDUCATION, LABOR, AND PENSIONS,
Washington, DC.

The committee met, pursuant to notice, at 10:04 a.m. in room SD–430, Dirksen Senate Office Building, Hon. Tom Harkin, chairman of the committee, presiding.

Present: Senators Harkin, Alexander, Burr, and Roberts.

OPENING STATEMENT OF SENATOR HARKIN

The CHAIRMAN. The Senate Committee on Health, Education, Labor, and Pensions will come to order.

We have convened this hearing this morning to examine the animal drug and animal generic drug user fee agreements that are due to be reauthorized this year. The Animal Drug User Fee Agreement, called ADUFA, and the Animal Generic Drug User Fee Agreement, called AGDUFA; we have a lot of "UFA's" around here. These programs mirror the fee programs for human medical products that this committee shepherded through the Senate last Congress as part of the FDA Safety and Innovation Act.

Both ADUFA and AGDUFA allow FDA to collect user fees from sponsors of animal drug and animal generic drug applications, and the Agency uses those fees to help fund the review of animal drug applications.

At today's hearing, we will discuss the history and purpose of these agreements between FDA and the animal drug industries that it regulates. We will delve into the agreements themselves to better understand the revenue that the fees provide and the performance standards that will benefit the industries paying those fees.

We will also learn about the importance of animal drug user fees to ensure that both pioneer and generic animal drugs are approved in a timely way. A fast, predictable approval of animal drugs, and their generic equivalents, benefits both the animals themselves and the people who depend on them.

As was true of the user fees for human medical products, both ADUFA and AGDUFA are negotiated between FDA and the industry subject to the fees, and we will hear today from the parties involved in those negotiations.

(1)

On our first panel, we will hear from Dr. Bernadette Dunham, the Director of FDA's Center for Veterinary Medicine. Dr. Dunham will discuss the critical role that the ADUFA and AGDUFA fees play in helping the Center for Veterinary Medicine ensure that animal drugs are safe and effective, and that they are made available as quickly as possible.

On the second panel, we will hear from the organizations that negotiated with FDA to reach these agreements that we are considering. In the negotiations with FDA, the pioneer animal drug industry was primarily represented by the Animal Health Institute. We have Dr. Richard Carnevale, AHI's vice president for Regulatory, Scientific, and International Affairs will discuss the past successes of the ADUFA program and the features of the new agreement.

He will be joined on the panel by Ms. Jennifer Johansson, the vice chair of the Generic Animal Drug Alliance. This Alliance represented the generic animal drug industry during these negotiations. And Ms. Johansson will talk to us about her industry's experience with the AGDUFA program and about the new agreement.

The testimony of today's witnesses will reflect consensus that the animal drug user fee programs are essential to FDA's timely review of pioneer and generic animal drugs. The agreements were carefully negotiated and it is important that we pass them this year.

I will leave the record open at this point for any opening statements by Senator Alexander when Senator Alexander arrives. He is just held up a little bit.

The CHAIRMAN. On our first panel, I would like to then invite to take the witness stand, Dr. Bernadette Dunham, the Director of the Center for Veterinary Medicine at the Food and Drug Administration. In this position, she works to foster animal and public health by ensuring the availability of safe and effective animal products. Dr. Dunham has over three decades of experience working in veterinary medicine, both in private practice and academia, and with the FDA.

Welcome to the committee, Dr. Dunham. Your statement will be made a part of the record in its entirety. If you could take 5 minutes or so to sum it up, I would appreciate it.

Welcome. Please proceed.

STATEMENT OF BERNADETTE M. DUNHAM, D.V.M., Ph.D., DIRECTOR, CENTER FOR VETERINARY MEDICINE, FOOD AND DRUG ADMINISTRATION, SILVER SPRING, MD

Ms. DUNHAM. Thank you. Good morning, Chairman Harkin.

I am Dr. Bernadette Dunham, Director of the Center for Veterinary Medicine at the Food and Drug Administration. Thank you for the opportunity to discuss FDA's proposals for the reauthorization of the Animal Drug User Fee and the Animal Generic Drug User Fee Act.

As you know, these fee programs are designed to expedite access to new therapies for food-producing animals and companion animals, and foster innovation in drug development by enabling FDA to maintain a stable workforce to provide a predictable and timely review process.

These programs have been highly successful and have enabled FDA to eliminate a backlog in applications, dramatically reduce the time needed to review animal drug applications and other submissions, improve timely communication with drug sponsors, and achieve other efficiencies in the drug-approval process while still ensuring the drugs are safe and effective.

In my testimony today, I will provide the status of FDA's reauthorization activities. I will also provide some information about each program, our achievements to date, and our proposed changes.

The user fee provisions, of ADUFA II and AGDUFA I, will sunset on October 1, 2013 if not reauthorized. Timely reauthorization is needed to ensure there is no disruption to these important programs.

FDA began the reauthorization process with a public meeting held on November 7, 2011 and began discussions with stakeholders in February 2012. FDA published the negotiated recommendations in the Federal Register on December 5, 2012 and posted for public comment. Another public meeting, to get input on the recommendations, was held December 18, 2012. The final recommendations transmitted to Congress include, for each program, the goals letter outlining the performance metrics, the proposed legislative language, and a summary of the public comments.

FDA considers the timely review of the safety and effectiveness of new animal drug applications to be central to the Agency's mission to protect and promote public health.

Under the original Animal Drug User Fee Act enacted in 2003, the Agency agreed to meet a comprehensive set of performance goals established to show significant improvement in the timeliness and predictability of the new animal drug review process.

The additional funding enabled FDA to increase the number of review staff by approximately 30 percent. In 2008, before ADUFA I expired, Congress passed ADUFA II, which included an extension of the program for an additional 5 years. And I am pleased to report that FDA has exceeded all of the performance goals established under ADUFA for each year of this critical program.

During the first 5 years of the program, the Agency was able to dramatically reduce review times from 500 to 180 days, and completely eliminate a backlog of 833 submissions within the first year. Due to the current success of the program, FDA and industry agree that only minor refinements to the performance goals that ADUFA II established were necessary.

Our recommendations relating to the financial enhancements of the program include a new statutory inflation adjuster, a new provision for recovering collection shortfalls, and modification of the workload adjuster. To increase revenue stream availability, reduce application fee costs, and minimize potential for collection shortfalls, the recommendations also modify the fee revenue distribution.

FDA's recommendation to Congress, after consultation with the regulated industry, is that the total fee revenue estimate for 2014 will be $23.6 million, which includes a one-time information technology funding in the amount of $2 million.

AGDUFA I authorized FDA's first-ever generic animal drug user fee program, and additional funding enabled FDA to increase the number of review staff by approximately 45 percent. Furthermore, the authorization of AGDUFA I enabled FDA's assurance that generic animal drug products are safe and effective to provide pet owners, ranchers, and farmers with greater access to lower cost therapeutic drugs. FDA agreed to meet performance goals and expedite the review of generic applications and submissions without compromising the quality of the Agency's review.

During the 4 years of AGDUFA I, FDA has exceeded every performance goal every year with one minor exception. We missed a performance goal by 1 day for one submission of an investigational generic and animal drug in 2009.

The additional resources provided under AGDUFA I enabled FDA to completely eliminate a backlog of 680 submissions in 22 months. In addition, the Agency has been able to dramatically reduce review times from 700 days to 270 days.

FDA's goals for AGDUFA II are to sustain and enhance the core programs, operation, and performance while providing predictable review times and resources sufficient to keep pace with actual costs. FDA and industry agree to shorter review times for certain reactivations and resubmissions, and to implement a process for timely foreign inspections.

Our recommendations for financial enhancements for AGDUFA II include a fixed inflation adjuster of 4 percent each year to achieve the proposed revenue levels, and a modification of the workload adjuster to ensure that it adequately captures FDA's workload. We also recommend modifying the fee revenue distribution to increase stability of the revenue stream and to reduce application fee costs.

The total 5-year revenue for AGDUFA I was $27.1 million. The proposed total 5-year revenue for AGDUFA II will be $38.1 million, which also includes a one-time IT funding of $850,000 for fiscal year 2014, the first year planned total of $7.328 million.

FDA's ADUFA and AGDUFA legislative proposals represent considerable input from an agreement of stakeholders, the public, and the Agency. ADUFA and AGDUFA are widely regarded as extremely successful programs. The recommendations we have submitted for reauthorization of these programs will ensure FDA has a stable workforce to provide the predictability and timely review process that drug sponsors need in order to foster innovation. They will also provide for expedited access to new therapies for food-producing animals and companion animals, while still ensuring the drugs are safe and effective.

Thank you for the opportunity to discuss the ADUFA and AGDUFA programs, and I look forward to your questions.

[The prepared statement of Ms. Dunham follows:]

PREPARED STATEMENT OF BERNADETTE M. DUNHAM, D.V.M., PH.D.

INTRODUCTION

Good morning, Chairman Harkin, Ranking Member Alexander, and members of the committee. I am Dr. Bernadette Dunham, Director of the Center for Veterinary Medicine (CVM) at the Food and Drug Administration (FDA or the Agency), which is part of the Department of Health and Human Services (HHS). Thank you for the opportunity to discuss FDA's proposals for the reauthorization of the Animal Drug User Fee Act (ADUFA III) and the Animal Generic Drug User Fee Act (AGDUFA II).

As you know, these fee programs are designed to expedite access to new therapies for food-producing animals and companion animals and foster innovation in drug development by enabling FDA to maintain a stable workforce to provide a predictable and timely review process. These programs have been highly successful and have enabled FDA to eliminate a backlog in applications, dramatically reduce the time needed to review animal drug applications and other submissions, improve timely communications with drug sponsors, and achieve other efficiencies in the drug approval process, while still ensuring that the drugs are safe and effective.

In my testimony today, I will provide the status of FDA's reauthorization activities. I will also provide some information about each program, our achievements to date, and our proposed changes.

STATUS OF FDA'S REAUTHORIZATION ACTIVITIES

The user fee provisions of ADUFA II and AGDUFA I will sunset on October 1, 2013, if not reauthorized. Timely reauthorization is needed to ensure there is no disruption to these important programs. FDA began the reauthorization process with a public meeting held on November 7, 2011. In February 2012, FDA began discussions to get input from our stakeholders to help us develop our recommendations for reauthorization. FDA consulted with representatives of patient and consumer advocacy groups, veterinary professionals, scientific and academic experts, and industry associations. FDA then published the negotiated recommendations in the *Federal Register* (FR) on December 5, 2012, and solicited public comment. We also held a second public meeting to get input on the recommendations on December 18, 2012. The final recommendations transmitted to Congress include, for each program, the goals letter outlining the performance metrics, the proposed legislative language, and a summary of public comments.

ADUFA BACKGROUND

FDA considers the timely review of the safety and effectiveness of new animal drug applications (NADA) to be central to the Agency's mission to protect and promote public health. One way we protect animal and human health is by approving safe and effective and properly labeled new animal drugs. Prior to 2004, the timeliness and predictability of the new animal drug review program was a concern. The original Animal Drug User Fee Act enacted in 2003 (ADUFA I) authorized FDA to collect user fees that were to be dedicated to expediting the review of NADAs in accordance with certain performance goals and to expand and modernize the new animal drug review program. The Agency agreed, under ADUFA I, to meet a comprehensive set of performance goals established to show significant improvement in the timeliness and predictability of the new animal drug review process. The implementation of ADUFA I provided a significant funding increase that enabled FDA to increase the number of staff dedicated to the review of animal drug applications by approximately 30 percent since 2003.

In 2008, before ADUFA I expired, Congress passed ADUFA II, which included an extension of the program for an additional 5 years (fiscal year 2009 to fiscal year 2013), as well as several enhancements to the program.

ADUFA ACHIEVEMENTS

I am pleased to report that FDA has exceeded all of the performance goals established under ADUFA for each year of this critical program. Under the performance goals of ADUFA, FDA agreed to review and act on submissions within shorter periods of time each successive year. During the first 5 years of this program, the Agency was able to dramatically reduce review times from 500 days to 180 days and completely eliminate a backlog of 833 submissions within the first year.

With ADUFA II, FDA agreed to further enhance the review process. A key improvement under ADUFA II is the "end-review amendment" (ERA) process that allows FDA reviewers to work with the drug sponsor to amend certain pending submissions. By enhancing communication early in the process, the ERA process allows FDA to decrease the number of review cycles, which ultimately leads to a shorter time to approval and significant cost-savings for the sponsor. The greatest impact of this new tool has been with submissions of investigational new animal drug (INAD) studies and study protocols. Greater than 90 percent of ERAs resulted in a favorable outcome in the first cycle.

Also as part of ADUFA II, FDA developed an electronic submission tool, which has enabled sponsors to submit applications and submissions electronically, allowing FDA reviewers to evaluate the submissions and correspond with sponsors electronically. Electronic submissions have provided substantial cost savings for both FDA and animal drug sponsors. Approximately 18 percent of submissions were electronic in 2011, the program's first year, and over 50 percent were electronic in 2012. Submissions are received by FDA in minutes rather than days, and correspondence back to sponsors occurs in minutes rather than the several days required for mailing responses.

Further, FDA and the regulated industry participated in eight joint public workshops on mutually agreed-upon topics. This collaboration enhanced communication and transparency on topics critical to the animal drug review process. The workshops discussed in detail the data requirements necessary for drug evaluation and explored scientific approaches to challenges in pharmacokinetics, new emerging issues relative to antiparasitic resistance, and a novel question-based-review (QbR) process for certain reviews. The final two public workshops for fiscal year 2013 will address the evaluation of drugs for use in animal production and data quality for animal drug submissions from sponsors.

ADUFA II also enabled FDA to improve the animal drug review and business processes by facilitating the timely scheduling and conducting of foreign preapproval inspections. Because of processes developed under ADUFA II, sponsors are now able to voluntarily submit an annual facilities list and notification 30 days prior to submitting an NADA, a supplemental NADA, or an INAD submission to inform FDA that the application or submission includes a foreign manufacturing facility. This advance notice gives FDA more time to plan for any necessary foreign inspections, thus helping to reduce costs and prevent delays during the review of an application or submission.

PROPOSAL FOR ADUFA III

FDA is proposing changes to the performance goals that ADUFA II established to further enhance the process for review of animal drug applications. Due to the current success of the program, FDA and industry agreed that only minor refinements were necessary.

The ERA procedure implemented as part of ADUFA II resulted in an increase in the number of one-cycle reviews; however, certain challenges associated with the process restricted its full utilization. The Agency is proposing, among other changes, to further improve the review process by replacing the ERA with shorter review times for certain resubmissions and reactivations beginning in fiscal year 2015. To allow time for the programming and information management system changes required to make this and other changes, we are proposing to maintain the ADUFA II ERA process and associated review performance goals for fiscal year 2014 for most applications.

FDA agrees to maintain the ADUFA II performance goals regarding work queue procedures, timely meetings with industry, review of administrative NADAs, and pre-approval foreign inspections. To enhance the exchange of scientific information, the Agency and industry agree on the need for industry to submit information earlier in development to enable the parties to reach agreement at a pre-submission conference or begin the review of study protocols. Additionally, FDA will provide increased flexibility for sponsors to submit scientific data or information concurrent with study protocol review.

Our recommendations relating to the financial enhancements of this program include a new statutory inflation adjuster that accounts for changes in FDA's costs related to payroll compensation and benefits as well as changes in non-payroll costs through use of a prescribed methodology that uses the Consumer Price Index as a guide. We also recommend modifying the base years for calculating the workload adjuster to ensure that it adequately captures changes in FDA's workload during ADUFA III.

Additionally, ADUFA III offers the following financial recommendations:

• A new provision for recovering collection shortfalls to ensure adequate funding for the animal drug review process. For example, when FDA sets fees for fiscal year 2016, it may add to the fee revenue the amount of any shortfall in fees collected in fiscal year 2014. This process would follow in subsequent years through the final year adjustment.

• A modified fee revenue distribution to increase revenue stream stability, reduce application fee costs, and minimize the potential for collection shortfalls. The proposed distribution will shift from 25 percent for each fee type in ADUFA II to 20 percent for application fees, 27 percent for product fees, 27 percent for sponsor fees, and 26 percent for establishment fees.

FDA's recommendation to Congress, after consultation with the regulated industry, is that the total fee revenue estimate for fiscal year 2014 will be $23,600,000, which includes one-time Information Technology (IT) funding in the amount of $2,000,000. The proposed statutory language specifies annual revenue of

$21,600,000 for each of fiscal year 2015 through fiscal year 2018; however, this amount is subject to a number of possible adjustments, including for inflation, workload, and collection shortfall.

AGDUFA BACKGROUND

AGDUFA I authorized FDA's first-ever generic animal drug user fee program. AGDUFA I provided a significant funding increase that enabled FDA to increase the number of staff dedicated to the new generic animal drug application review process by approximately 45 percent. Furthermore, the authorization of AGDUFA I enabled FDA's continued assurance that generic animal drug products are safe and effective and provided consumers with greater access to lower-cost therapeutic drugs.

Under AGDUFA I, FDA agreed to meet performance goals for certain submissions over 5 years from fiscal year 2009 through fiscal year 2013. The purpose of establishing these performance goals was to expedite the review of abbreviated new animal drug applications (ANADA) and reactivations, supplemental ANADAs, and generic investigational new animal drug (JINAD) submissions without compromising the quality of the Agency's review.

AGDUFA ACHIEVEMENTS

AGDUFA I established increasingly stringent review performance goals. In the 4 years of AGDUFA I review performance evaluated to date (fiscal year 2009 to fiscal year 2012), FDA has exceeded every performance goal every year with one minor exception. During the program's first year, the Agency missed the performance goal by 1 day for one submission of an investigational generic new animal drug. Most importantly, the additional resources provided under AGDUFA I enabled FDA to completely eliminate a backlog of 680 submissions in 22 months. In addition, the Agency has been able to dramatically reduce review times from 700 days to 270 days. The timely approval of generic new animal drugs continues to be a critical component of animal health because it provides quicker access to additional sources of animal drugs at lower cost for ranchers, farmers, and pet owners.

PROPOSAL FOR AGDUFA II

FDA's goals for the legislative proposal to reauthorize AGDUFA I are to sustain and enhance the core program's operation and performance while providing predictable review times and resources sufficient to keep pace with actual costs. The Agency is proposing to maintain the AGDUFA I goals regarding work queue procedures, timely meetings with industry, review of administrative ANADAs, review of protocols without substantial data, and amendments of similar applications and submissions.

FDA and industry agreed to shorter review times for certain reactivations and resubmissions. The Agency also agreed to increased communication and transparency with industry through timely meetings and question-based-review (QbR) for bioequivalence submissions, which are most often used when a sponsor proposes manufacturing a generic version of an approved off-patent product. The QbR incorporates the most important scientific and regulatory review questions that focus on critical pharmaceutical attributes essential for ensuring generic drug product quality. In addition, FDA further agreed to implement a process for timely foreign inspections as provided in ADUFA II.

Similar to AGDUFA I, our recommendations for financial enhancements for AGDUFA II include a fixed inflation adjuster of 4 percent each year to achieve the proposed revenue levels. We also recommend modifying the base years for calculating the workload adjuster to ensure that it adequately captures changes in FDA's workload during AGDUFA II. Additionally, the fee revenue distribution has been modified from 30 percent for application fees, 35 percent for product fees, and 35 percent for sponsor fees under AGDUFA I to 25 percent for application fees and 37.5 percent for both product fees and sponsor fees under AGDUFA II. The purpose of changing the fee distribution is to increase the stability of the revenue stream and reduce application fee costs.

The total 5-year revenue for AGDUFA I was $27,100,000. The proposed total 5-year revenue for AGDUFA II will be $38,100,000, which also includes one-time IT funding in the amount of $850,000 for fiscal year 2014 for a first-year planned total of $7,328,000.

CONCLUSION

FDA's ADUFA and AGDUFA legislative proposals represent considerable input from and agreement of stakeholders, the public, and the Agency. ADUFA and

AGDUFA are widely regarded as extremely successful programs. The recommendations we have submitted for reauthorization of these programs will ensure FDA has a stable workforce to provide the predictable and timely review process that drug sponsors need to foster innovation. They also will provide for expedited access to new therapies for food-producing animals and companion animals, while still ensuring that the drugs are safe and effective. FDA looks forward to working with you and your staff to achieve a timely reauthorization of these important human and animal health programs.

Thank you for the opportunity to discuss the ADUFA and AGDUFA programs. I would be happy to answer any questions.

The CHAIRMAN. Thank you very much, Dr. Dunham. And we will start a round of 5 minute questions.

My first is this: congratulations on reducing the amount of time for these applications, cut down in half on both ADUFA and AGDUFA. Can you assure us, and the public, that even with this reduction in time that safety has not been compromised?

Ms. DUNHAM. Yes, sir. I can assure you that our reviewers are very experienced, and our whole focus is absolutely to do what FDA does very well: assure the safety and effectiveness of these drugs through critical review, making sure the manufacturing and the labeling of these products is absolutely correct to ensure that safety.

The CHAIRMAN. But is the reduction in time that is taken due to the fact that because of the increased funding through the fees, you have been able to hire more staff, and that has enabled you to reduce that time, but still maintain the safety factor. Is that correct?

Ms. DUNHAM. That is correct, sir.

The CHAIRMAN. The point I'm trying to make is that the increased funding has allowed you to hire the competent staff in order to get the job done in a reduced amount of time.

Ms. DUNHAM. In reduced time and not be able to jeopardize anything on safety and effectiveness when we do the reviews. Yes, sir.

The CHAIRMAN. If we did not reauthorize ADUFA by October 1 of this year, and AGDUFA fees if we did not reauthorize these fees, briefly tell us what repercussions would that have for FDA and ultimately for animal and public health.

Ms. DUNHAM. The concern that we would have is that we would end up going back to the days that we have mentioned before. We would have longer review times. We would lose approximately about 100 of the staff that we have had an opportunity to hire through the ADUFA program, and that really would set us back. I would be very concerned that we would not be able to continue providing safe and effective drugs to address the animal health needs of the Nation.

The CHAIRMAN. And last, just briefly again, how do producers of food animals benefit from ADUFA and AGDUFA? Briefly, how do they benefit from this?

Ms. DUNHAM. They are going to benefit because part and parcel is to make sure we keep all of our animals healthy. And for that, to be able to access the safe and effective drugs, work with their veterinarians, as well as the generic animal drug side, which still allows them access to safe and effective drugs, sometimes at reduced cost, is something that helps them with their entire operation. So ensuring not only the health of the animals, but more importantly, any of the food items from those animals and that is their livelihood, of which we have a very important role in protecting public health and animal health.

The CHAIRMAN. Thank you very much, Dr. Dunham.

I will now yield to Senator Alexander.

STATEMENT OF SENATOR ALEXANDER

Senator ALEXANDER. Thanks, Mr. Chairman.

Just to go back over the point that you made and that the Chairman mentioned. You have reduced—you've got a 450-day reduction time in the average time you spend reviewing new drugs, and you have eliminated the backlog, is that right?

Ms. DUNHAM. Yes, sir, we have. Over the years that we have had, this is our second authorization period of ADUFA and it would be, sorry, this is our third; we have had it two times.

Over the 9 years, we have tremendously accomplished meeting all of our performance goals and having reduced that backlog, actually, during the very first authorization of ADUFA, and the same happened with AGDUFA, our generic drug fee user program. Once we had an opportunity to really get staff onboard, we managed to reduce the backlog.

Senator ALEXANDER. How many applications did you have in backlog when there was a backlog?

Ms. DUNHAM. We had over 700 that we managed to drop with that backlog when we had the staff.

Senator ALEXANDER. Go through the time sequence today. If I had an application for approval of a new drug, take me through the time sequence, about the average amount of time it might take.

Ms. DUNHAM. When a sponsor comes to us with their proposal, there are a number of aspects that have to be reviewed, and we have broken these down into technical sections. Based upon the time that it takes the company to come in with each one of these sections, that will determine the review time.

At the very end, when the entire package is ready to review, we are now meeting on the ADUFA side the statutory review time of 180 days. And the time that it takes is all dependent upon the complexity of that particular drug that we are reviewing.

Senator ALEXANDER. So you are within the 180 day statutory——

Ms. DUNHAM. Now we are. We were not before, and that is what this ADUFA fee program has enabled us over these years to meet, which has been a success story. And it really helps the companies because now they are going to have reliable performance goals with our steady increased stability of revenue to meet that, and to understand what it takes to get us there. And before that, there were a lot of delays and unknowns, and now we have managed to fine tune all of that and enhance this.

Senator ALEXANDER. And the 180 days, is it part of the proposal for the reauthorization?

Ms. DUNHAM. Yes, to sustain those performance review times.

Senator ALEXANDER. What is the greatest difficulty that applicants have in that period before you get all the documents? Do you get complaints about complexity or difficulty of providing that information? And if so, what are you doing about that?

Ms. DUNHAM. Actually, through the program, we have had an opportunity to work very closely in enhancing communication, working very closely with industry.

We have had 10 workshops scheduled; we have completed eight of them. Whereby you do have an opportunity to really have an exchange back and forth from our reviewers to the industry to fine tune some of the complexities that they are addressing in the review that we would like them to work with us on so that we enhance that clarity and expectations, and by doing that, fine tune so that everything comes through with a goal of one cycle review. And through those dialogs, we have really had a terrific——

Senator ALEXANDER. One cycle, you mean, so you don't have to send it back and start over.

Ms. DUNHAM. Right, exactly, and that is the whole purpose of enhanced communication. So that you are not caught with surprises, so we understand expectations. We do a tremendous amount now with——

Senator ALEXANDER. Do you catch them doing things wrong, or do you talk with them ahead of time and say, "Fill it out this way instead of that way,"?

Ms. DUNHAM. That is the open dialog so that there is a free exchange that we can go back and forth to understand if we have hit an issue or they have had a delay on something. So we know that and we can work that time into the plan.

Senator ALEXANDER. How many pending applications do you have or, however you measure, the number of applications that you are working on today?

Ms. DUNHAM. I would have to get back to you to give you that exact number. I don't know off the top of my head.

Senator ALEXANDER. I am just trying to get an idea of how much business you have in a year or how many applications you review in a year.

Ms. DUNHAM. Well, we have managed to basically, even over the past 9 years, we have had about 3,600 drugs and supplements be approved through ADUFA. And over the last 4 years of the program with AGDUFA, we have had about 500. So in that sense, some can be very complex new applications and innovative drugs, others can be a lot of supplements that we deal with as well.

Senator ALEXANDER. Well, Mr. Chairman, based upon what I have heard so far, maybe we ought to put them in charge of some other parts of the Government as well.

[Laughter.]

The CHAIRMAN. I will second that.

Ms. DUNHAM. Thank you very much.

[The prepared statement of Senator Alexander follows:]

PREPARED STATEMENT OF SENATOR ALEXANDER

Mr. Chairman, thank you for holding a hearing today on these successful programs. It has been 5 years since the last round of animal drug and animal generic drug user fee negotiations, and I look forward to hearing about the impact of the fees on animal drug approvals.

Keeping animals healthy is imperative for public health. And as we spend this morning learning more about the process and benefits of these two user fee programs I would like to tell a story about why the success of these programs is important.

I know a farmer in East Tennessee who buys calves from local livestock markets to raise on grass and grain. He checks on his calves two or more times per day. When he detects a calf that is not feeling well, he pulls him out of the group into another area where he gives him a drug.

How does this farmer know the calf isn't feeling well? He says it is like how you know your child is not feeling well. He says the calf just doesn't look "right". A calf might have droopy ears or his eyes might not be as bright.

This farmer needs to be able to have access to the proper drug in order to get his calves back healthy as quickly as possible. My constituent, along with 17,500 other Tennessee beef cattle farmers, has been Beef Quality Assurance Certified. This means that they have the proper training and knowledge to handle and administer animal drug products. This Tennessean wants to do all that he can do to produce a safe and wholesome product to feed not only to others, but also to his family.

Without access to safe and effective animal medicines that are also studied for their impact on the food supply, farmers would be severely hampered in their ability to help animals that become sick. So when we see the results of this program, such as a 450-day reduction in the average time the Food and Drug Administration (FDA) spends reviewing new generic animal drugs over the last 5 years, and that FDA has eliminated the backlog of 680 applications, that means improved care for animals and faster access to animal medicines for this farmer and many like him. Since the animal drug user fees have been in place many new products have been approved, including a product to control fever in pigs suffering from pneumonia and iron supplements for newborn piglets.

When discussing the technical details of the FDA and industry user fee agreement we need to keep in mind the people affected at the end of the process: the farmers and animal owners who use these products to keep their animals healthy and our food supply safe. We plan to mark up legislation on these agreements soon and hope to pass this quickly to ensure the staff at the Center for Veterinary Medicine can continue their good work. These are important agreements that Congress should reauthorize quickly without complications that could jeopardize swift passage of the bill. I hope that we keep the lessons from our last animal drug and animal generic drug user fee legislation in mind as we work on these important agreements. I thank Chairman Harkin for his leadership, commitment and look forward to learning more about the programs' success from today's witnesses.

The CHAIRMAN. Thank you.

Senator Burr.

STATEMENT OF SENATOR BURR

Senator BURR. Thank you, Mr. Chairman.

Dr. Dunham, congratulations on not only a great performance, but the ability to come up and have industry support for a reauthorization like this. I am curious, off of the Chairman's points to you, how have you been able to accomplish through ADUFA what you have, while user fees in other areas of FDA providing additional FTE's only increased the review time versus decrease the review time? What is different that you have done than the other areas at FDA?

Ms. DUNHAM. That is a very good question. I think we have always struggled to be as expeditious as we can. And this additional user fee program just made that opportunity of enhancing the wonderful staff that we have—their dedication is incredible—to be able to provide them with the tools they need. And having done that, the energy is there, and working with industry so that we are really striving to have this be as clear as we possibly can, to understand the challenges.

It has been a win across the board, and it is really through the availability of the dedicated staff that we have, and the opportune program you have provided which really helps us to——

Senator BURR. If I understand this reauthorization, there are no additional FTE's being hired.

Ms. DUNHAM. We are going to continue because we have managed to fine tune the process, and we have now also gone electronic. And I think that is the biggest boost in enhancing our review times now because we can suffice that so quickly electronically back and forth. That has given a tremendous advantage to us on obtaining the data and reviewing the data.

Senator BURR. Part of this agreement requires the industry to pay $2 million up front in one-time IT funding. What are the specific goals that you have for that $2 million worth of IT payment? And what are the benchmarks that the Agency will use to track the success of these goals?

Ms. DUNHAM. Where we are going to be using the dollars for IT, as we have mentioned, moving into electronic submission form, a number of the various codes and software coordination of that documentation requires us to work with the IT folks to make those changes in the business process. So that when a reviewer receives a supplement, you code it in, coordination of the technical sections, all of that needed to fine tune now with the business operation.

We took advantage of requesting and working with the industry because now that we are moving electronically, we needed to make a few changes, literally, that only IT could handle. And it is more or less just fine tuning the business process side of that, and it is just changing some of those codes that we have.

Senator BURR. Dr. Carnevale says in his testimony that increases in regulatory costs and burden are contributing to a declining number of new animal drug approvals. As CVM Director, what are you and your staff doing to increase the regulatory certainty and predictability of the Agency and to decrease regulatory costs and burden, which have had somewhat of a chilling effect on innovation? Or, would you agree with that?

Ms. DUNHAM. I think any time we are facing challenges of finances that does, and that is really why this user fee program has acknowledged how to help our industry come forth with, still, the innovative products that we need. By minimizing, potentially, having multiple cycles is a benefit to them, so that you are not going to have additional costs; that is a win.

13

That enhanced communication that we talked about, so there is clarity of what we are striving to obtain, has really minimized it. We also have an opportunity for waivers. If we have some small businesses that are coming onboard, we have worked through the user fee program to acknowledge that and assist them. So anything that flags up as a potential barrier to innovation, we put a waiver in because we understand how important that is to continue to support them.

On the generic user fee program, we've also got a three-tier program. Again, trying to work with our companies, understanding where they are. Some of them are not multiple, big applications. And I think that fairness, and listening to them, and working through that is how we both work together.

That is another reason why, as you asked originally, what is part of our success story? It is really trying to understand that we all want to ensure safe and effective drugs, and to understand what it takes to have the industry come in the front door, and for us to do those reviews and work with them.

Senator BURR. Part of this agreement deals with conditional approvals, and it is for the Agency to explore in concert with the industry the feasibility of pursuing statutory revisions that may expand that use of conditional approvals. Yet, there is not much specificity in how that is going to happen. Can you sort of explain to me what the matrix is that we should look at to see if this is successful or not?

Ms. DUNHAM. This was actually started with our minor use minor species animal drug development program whereby, you can imagine, we may not have sufficient numbers and I will give you a simple example, going to the zoo animals.

How many elephants would we have, how many tigers if we want to get this drug reviewed for safety and effectiveness? So we may be able to get all of the safety done, first and foremost. But the effectiveness, do we have sufficient numbers of those animals? We may then allow the company to take a little bit longer to access the effectiveness data just because they may not have sufficient numbers.

Senator BURR. Under a conditional approval?

Ms. DUNHAM. Under a conditional approval, and so the safety has to be there. The only layer of the conditional approval is fine tuning the last bit of the effectiveness. And that has been a tremendous asset to help with those products as we have seen them coming through for minor species.

So the scenario was: is there a venue possibly? Could we look at that for some areas in our major species? This is just to take a look and see, is there any possibility that that could be another way of helping to, again, take a look at the cost of the drug review, the timing, and some of the more challenging issues, would that work or not?

There is no guarantee, but it has been a very successful program on the minor use species side. We thought, they asked. I think it is very good that we always try to embrace new ideas and let's see if this is going to work.

Senator BURR. Great. Thank you.

Thank you, Mr. Chairman.

Ms. DUNHAM. Thank you.
The CHAIRMAN. Senator Roberts.

STATEMENT OF SENATOR ROBERTS

Senator ROBERTS. Thank you, Mr. Chairman. Thank you for holding the hearing. Dr. Dunham, I may nominate you for the Freedom Medal; that's a pretty prestigious award. I don't know of anybody else in the regulatory business—and virtually every agency that we have in the Government today—who has done a better job than you in following the law. Mr. Chairman, just let me go down the list.

First, these folks had public hearings. So people came in from the antibiotic arena, said what they had to say, made suggestions. Then these folks had an Advanced Notice of Proposed Rule Making; the acronym for that is ANPRM. I did not know that, A-N-P-R-M. I thought it was something that you took.

[Laughter.]

Senator ROBERTS. Which, in this case, is probably a common-sense pill to get the cost benefit worked out and really let people know. So that was a heads up.

First you had the hearings. They testified. Then you had a heads up on Advanced Notice of Proposed Rule Making. Then you had a notice of proposed rulemaking, which we are into right now. So after hearing from the public and then giving them an advanced notice of what you have in mind, now we have a notice of proposed rulemaking and you are getting feedback. Then you go to the final rule. OK? And I would tell my colleagues, and I want to thank you, that this is the way it is supposed to work.

That over a period of time that is appropriate that you tell the industry, or you ask the industry, "Is this going to work? Is there a better way we can do it? Maybe we can tweak it, maybe not." But you have done all that. As opposed to almost virtually every other agency that my colleagues and I wrestle with, trying to make some kind of a cost-benefit criteria apply, even though we have an Executive order that says that that is the case, it is not happening.

Classic case is with regards to PPACA or the Affordable Care Act, where the rules have gone to OMB and they are final. But upon questions, CMS will tell us that, "Well, we've talked to all the providers," and that is a long list of providers in terms of health care.

On sub-regulatory guidance, the problem is nobody knows about the sub-regulatory guidance. You don't operate that way. You are going out to the people going to be affected and trying to get a better sense in regards to the regulations that you are issuing. That is why we have a clean bill.

And the sub-regulatory guidelines can now be bulletins. Who has time to look at bulletins? How do you get a hold of the bulletins if you are a small, rural hospital in Kansas, Tennessee, Iowa, wherever, North Carolina? You don't have time. How do you gain access to the bulletins? Well, it is on their Web site. Well, who is going to be the bad-news-bearer sitting there at the hospital looking at bulletins every day?

You have Frequently Asked Questions, I love that, FAQ, frequently asked questions. Boy, there's a bunch of those. And so,

15

they get the questions and then they come back and say, "Here's a bunch of frequently asked questions," but I am not sure that they really answer the questions.

Then you have a Web site, of course, and then you finally have guidance documents. So I guess, if you ask guidance on a particular item, they will send you a document on their Web site and you're supposed to wade through that.

You don't have an ambulance driver, a hospice director, a home health care person, a nurse, a doctor, a hospital, everybody that receives Medicare, and I am just picking on that because it is an example. And then you have regs going over to OMB, and I suspect that this committee does not know all of the ramifications of those, we will. But with the Chairman's leadership, that is for sure, and we are doing the same thing in the finance committee.

But you, doctor, have done it the right way, and I want to congratulate you for that.

Ms. DUNHAM. Thank you.

Senator ROBERTS. Because we need regulatory framework to protect the public, and you are doing that, but you are asking the industry, "How can we do it in the best possible way?" Now that is a long speech, but I think you deserve a big pat on the back.

Mr. Chairman and Ranking Member, thank you for having a clean bill, and if we have a clean bill with appropriate comment, that is what we are supposed to be doing. So thank you both, and thank you, doctor.

Ms. DUNHAM. Thank you very much. I really appreciate that.

The CHAIRMAN. Thank you, Senator Roberts. Well, I hope we can keep it a clean bill as it weaves its way through that place over there in the Capitol called the Senate floor. I hope we can keep it clean.

Dr. Dunham, thank you very much.

Ms. DUNHAM. Thank you very, very much.

The CHAIRMAN. We will call our second panel, Dr. Richard Carnevale and Dr. Jennifer Johansson.

Mr. CARNEVALE. Good morning.

The CHAIRMAN. The second panel of the committee has invited Dr. Richard Carnevale, the vice president for Regulatory, Scientific, and International Affairs with the Animal Health Institute, an animal pharmaceutical trade association. Dr. Carnevale has worked for 35 years in the animal health and food safety industry, and has previously held positions with both the FDA and USDA, and holds a doctorate in veterinary medicine from the University of Pennsylvania.

Also Jennifer Johansson, the vice chair of the Generic Animal Drug Alliance. In addition to her role with GADA, Ms. Johansson is the senior vice president of Putney Generic Veterinary Pharmaceuticals where she leads their regulatory affairs efforts. Ms. Johansson has 16 years of experience in the pharmaceutical and research industry including physicians in a human specialty pharmaceutical company in private legal practice, and is a laboratory researcher at NIH.

We thank you both for being here. Your statements will be made a part of the record in their entirety. We will start with you, Dr. Carnevale. Welcome. Please proceed.

STATEMENT OF RICHARD A. CARNEVALE, V.M.D., VICE PRESIDENT, REGULATORY, SCIENTIFIC AND INTERNATIONAL AFFAIRS, ANIMAL HEALTH INSTITUTE, WASHINGTON, DC

Mr. CARNEVALE. Good morning. Thank you, Mr. Chairman and members of the committee. Thank you for holding this hearing on this important piece of legislation, and the opportunity to speak to you today about the important human and animal health benefits that result from using medicines to keep animals healthy.

I am Dr. Richard Carnevale. I am a veterinarian by training with a degree from the University of Pennsylvania School of Veterinary Medicine. And I am here today on behalf of the Animal Health Institute, the trade association that represents companies that make medicines for animals.

Our companies share a common mission: we contribute to public health by protecting animal health. Animal health products also give veterinarians, and livestock, and poultry producers the necessary tools to protect the health and well-being of food-producing animals.

Veterinarians work hard to prevent disease in animals, but it is important for them to have medicines available when needed to treat a disease or disease threat. The FDA animal drug approval process looks much like the human drug approval process. Animal drug companies submit data packages to demonstrate safety, efficacy, and the ability to meet the same stringent FDA manufacturing standards.

It is a costly process requiring as much as $100 million, and 7 to 10 years to bring an animal drug to market. The market for animal drugs, however, is nothing like the market for human drugs. Our products are used to treat seven different major species of animals and many more minor species. A blockbuster animal drug is considered one with sales of around $100 million with the vast majority of animal health products averaging about $1 million or less in gross sales. There is no Medicare or Medicaid, and except in rare cases, no employer-supported health insurance. The cost of animal drugs is primarily borne fully by the animal owner.

Passage of this legislation will have important benefits. FDA-CVM benefits by having additional resource needs to meet its mission of protecting public health. Animal health sponsors benefit from a stable and predictable review process allowing them to make more informed decisions about the investment risks of research and development dollars.

Veterinarians benefit from having new and innovative medical advances available to treat, control, and prevent diseases in their patients. And livestock and poultry producers and the veterinarians on whose advice they rely, also have the tools needed to keep food animals healthy.

And pet owners, let's not forget them, will benefit by having their animals live longer and healthier lives, increasing their enjoyment of these companions.

And finally consumers reap the food safety benefits that come as a result of the availability of additional tools to keep food animals healthy.

AHI believes that the funding agreed to by the industry over the next 5 years is based on an objective assessment of Agency resource needs, and will allow the Agency to maintain all current standards, and also improve performance in key areas. The agreement calls for approximately $118 million in funding over the 5 years and uses a variable rather than a fixed inflation factor.

The financial agreement seeks to reduce the impact that fees may have on small businesses and smaller product markets by reducing the total percentage of fees coming from new animal drug applications and supplements from 25 percent to 20 percent. This agreement also includes a provision for FDA to make up potential fee shortfalls that may be experienced by allowing for adjustments to levied fees in the out years of the program.

FDA has consistently met all timeframes for all sentinel submissions identified in the goals letter that was submitted to Congress the past two ADUFA's, and we are confident that the Agency will continue to do so over the next 5 fiscal years.

The new agreement continues all current submission review timeframes mandated in ADUFA II. However, the new agreement adds important enhancements to the review process.

Animal drugs generally go through a phased review process, which is different from human drugs whereby each specific area called technical sections of the new animal drug application are submitted and reviewed independently. Once the technical sections for safety, efficacy, manufacturing, and environmental impact are complete, an administrative NADA is filed referencing those sections, and approval of the product occurs within 60 days.

If technical sections can be completed more rapidly, it will lead to earlier filing of the administrative NADA, and therefore reduce overall time to the marketing of safe and effective animal medicines. This will be accomplished under the new agreement by FDA agreeing to significantly shorten the review times of the second pass submissions that ordinarily are reviewed in the same timeframe as the original or first pass submissions. Now that will occur when certain criteria in the goals letter are met.

Depending on the type of submission, this can result in up to a 4-month or 120-day decreased review time, which is very important and could be critical in moving an important medicine to market sooner. The new agreement also commits the Agency to work with the industry to examine longer term goals. First, AHI and FDA will enter into discussions on how to more broadly extend the conditional approval process currently available for all practical purposes only to minor species to major species applications.

Second, FDA will enter into a discussion with the animal drug and feed industry, and State regulatory authorities overseeing animal feed, to determine how requirements for combination medicated feed approvals might be modified.

This could have a significant future importance with the advent of the FDA proposal to move more antimicrobials used in feed to a Veterinary Feed Directive program by allowing veterinarians to more efficiently write VFD orders for antibiotics to be mixed into feed with other non-VFD drugs. Eliminating the requirement for combination feed approvals could pave the way for a smoother implementation of the VFD program, and ensure that antimicrobials that are added to feed are being used for therapeutic purposes only under the order of a veterinarian.

Mr. Chairman, CVM has a rigorous science-based approval process that provides to the American public the products necessary to protect public health by protecting animal health. Every year, scientists uncover new diseases in animals, some of which potentially pose a threat to human health. As more animals are raised to feed the planet, and as animals are reared closer to people, we will continue to need new medicines to protect animal and human health.

The reauthorization of ADUFA will continue to provide the Agency the resources necessary to maintain and improve this approval process, provide new and innovative products to allow our pets to live longer and healthier lives, and contribute to food safety by keeping food animals healthy.

I urge you to move a clean ADUFA bill in a timely manner so this program can continue without interruption.

Thank you, Mr. Chairman. I would be happy to take questions.
[The prepared statement of Mr. Carnevale follows:]

PREPARED STATEMENT OF RICHARD A. CARNEVALE, V.M.D.

SUMMARY

The Animal Health Institute (AHI) is the trade association representing research-based companies that make medicines for animals, both companion animals and farm animals.

Passage of the Animal Drug User Fee Act will assist FDA's Center for Veterinary Medicine by providing additional resources to meet its mission of protecting public health. Animal health sponsors benefit from a stable and predictable review process, allowing them to make more informed decisions about the investment risks of research and development dollars. Veterinarian and animal owners benefit from a critical supply of new and innovative medicines to keep animals healthy. Consumers reap the food safety benefits that come as a result of the availability of additional tools to keep food animals healthy.

The funding agreement, based on an objective assessment of agency resource needs, calls for approximately $118 million in funding over the 5 years, and uses a variable rather than fixed inflation factor. The financial agreement seeks to reduce the impact that fees may have on small businesses and smaller product markets by reducing the total percentage of fees coming from new animal drug applications and supplements from 25 percent to 20 percent. The agreement also includes a provision for FDA to make up potential fee shortfalls that may be experienced by allowing for adjustments to levied fees in the out years of the program.

The new agreement continues all current submission review timeframes mandated in ADUFA II. One enhancement added by this agreement is to significantly shorten the review times of the second pass submissions that ordinarily are reviewed in the same timeframe as the original or first pass submissions, when certain criteria in the goals letter are met. Depending on the type of submission this can result in up to a 4-month (120 day) decreased review time and could be critical in moving an important animal medicine to the market sooner.

The new agreement also commits the agency to work with industry to examine longer term goals: First, AHI and FDA will enter into discussions on how to more broadly extend the conditional approval process currently available only to minor species to major species applications. Second, FDA will enter into discussion with the animal drug and animal feed industry and State regulatory authorities overseeing animal feed to determine how requirements for combination medicated feed approvals might be modified. Eliminating the requirement for combination feed approvals could pave the way for a smoother implementation of the VFD program and ensure that antimicrobials added to feed are being used for therapeutic purposes only under the order of a veterinarian.

The reauthorization of ADUFA will continue to provide the agency the resources necessary to maintain and improve this approval process, provide new and innovative products to allow our pets to live longer and healthier lives and contribute to food safety by keeping food animals healthy. AHI urges Congress to move a clean ADUFA bill in a timely manner so this program can continue without interruption.

Mr. Chairman and members of the committee, thank you for holding this hearing on this important piece of legislation, and for the opportunity to speak to you today about the important human and animal health benefits that result from using medicines to keep animals healthy.

I am Dr. Richard Carnevale. I am a veterinarian by training with a degree from the University of Pennsylvania and I am here today on behalf of the Animal Health Institute (AHI), a trade association that represents companies that make medicines for animals. Our companies share a common mission: we contribute to public health by protecting animal health. With food animals in more demand from our growing global population, the importance of the nexus between animal health and human health has never been greater, and is one of the driving forces behind the Center for Disease Control's "One Health" initiative. As companion animals have become a more important part of our everyday lives they have moved from the backyard into our living rooms and bedrooms, increasing their importance to humans and requiring greater attention to their health needs. As medical breakthroughs from human medicine are adapted to animal medicine, our pets are living longer and healthier lives.

Animal health products also give veterinarians, and livestock and poultry producers, the necessary tools to protect the health and well-being of food producing animals. More and more evidence demonstrates that a vital first step in producing safe meat, milk and eggs is keeping animals healthy. Veterinarians work hard to prevent disease in animals, but it is important for them to have medicines available when needed to treat a disease or disease threat.

The statutory standard for FDA approval of animal drugs under the Federal Food, Drug and Cosmetic Act is the same as that for human drugs: they must be proven to be safe and effective. As a result, the animal drug approval process looks much like the human drug approval process: animal drug companies submit data packages to demonstrate safety, efficacy, and the ability to meet the same stringent FDA manufacturing standards. It is a costly process, requiring as much as $100 million and 7–10 years to bring an animal drug to market. In the case of food animals, the standard to ensure that meat, milk, and eggs are safe for human consumption adds an additional set of requirements that increases the cost and time to market.

The market for animal drugs, however, is nothing like the market for human drugs. Our products are used to treat seven different major species of animals and many more minor species. A blockbuster animal drug will have sales of $100 million, and the vast majority of animal health products have a market size of around $1 million. There is no Medicare or Medicaid and, except in rare cases, no employer-supported health insurance—the cost of animal drugs is borne in full by the animal owner.

One significant challenge we face in animal health is the declining number of new animal drug approvals. The data we collected in preparation for ADUFA III clearly showed that while we significantly increased the amount of user fees going to the agency in ADUFA II, the workload has substantially declined. There are likely many reasons for this, but a big reason is the ever-increasing regulatory cost and burden. In a market as fractured as the animal health market, this increased regulatory burden results in fewer live-saving and extending drugs being brought to market. We hope Congress will consider ways to incentivize animal health research and provide for a regulatory environment that increases the availability of animal health products.

Animal health companies rely on a rigorous, efficient, predictable and science-based review process at the Food and Drug Administration's Center for Veterinary Medicine (CVM) to provide these products. That's why our companies supported the first authorization of the Animal Drug User Fee Act 10 years ago. The Animal Drug User Fee Act of 2003 (ADUFA I) made it possible for our companies to bolster funding at CVM so that they could meet performance standards to improve the efficiency and predictability of the animal drug approval process and ADUFA II, passed in 2008, continued that progress.

Passage of this important legislation will have several benefits:

1. FDA/CVM benefits by having additional resources to meet its mission of protecting public health.

2. Animal health sponsors benefit from a stable and predictable review process, allowing them to make informed decisions about the investment risks of research and development dollars.

3. Veterinarians benefit from having new and innovative medical advances available to treat, control and prevent diseases in their patients.

4. Livestock and poultry producers, and the veterinarians on whose advice they rely, also have the tools needed to keep food animals healthy.

5. Pet owners benefit by having their animals live longer and healthier lives, increasing their enjoyment of these companions.

6. Consumers reap the food safety benefits that come as a result of the availability of additional tools to keep food animals healthy.

AHI believes that the funding agreed to by the industry over the next 5 years is based on an objective assessment of agency resource needs and will allow the agency to maintain all current standards and also improve performance in key areas. The agreement calls for approximately $118 million in funding over the 5 years, depending on inflation. The funding agreement going forward differs from the funding provided over the last 5 years. AHI has agreed to an annual fee level adjusted by a variable rather than the fixed annual inflation factor utilized in ADUFA II. The variable rate will be more closely aligned with actual cost increases that FDA might realize from year to year.

The financial agreement seeks to reduce the impact that fees may have on small businesses and smaller product markets by reducing the total percentage of fees coming from new animal drug applications and supplements from 25 percent to 20 percent. This should result in a substantial reduction in an individual application fee in fiscal year 2014 and beyond. The 5 percent reduction is then distributed among the three remaining fee areas—sponsor, product and establishment. Since smaller companies have fewer products and facilities, they are hit hardest by the application fee. The agreement also includes a provision for FDA to make up potential fee shortfalls that may be experienced by allowing for adjustments to levied fees in the out years of the program.

FDA has consistently met timeframes for all sentinel submissions identified in the goals letter submitted to Congress and we are confident that the agency will continue to do so over the next 5 fiscal years. The new agreement continues all current submission review timeframes mandated in ADUFA II. However, the new agreement adds important enhancements to the review process.

The process for reviewing and approving animal drugs has evolved over the years and is somewhat different than that for human medicines. Animal drugs generally go through a phased review process whereby each specific area called technical sections of the new animal drug application is submitted and reviewed independently. Once the technical sections for safety, efficacy, manufacturing, and environmental impact are complete an administrative NADA is filed referencing those sections and approval of the product occurs within 60 days.

If technical sections can be completed more rapidly it will lead to earlier filing of the administrative NADA and, therefore, reduce overall time to market of safe and effective animal medicines. This will be accomplished under the new agreement by FDA agreeing to significantly shorten the review times of the second pass submissions that ordinarily are reviewed in the same timeframe as the original or first pass submissions, when certain criteria in the goals letter are met. Depending on the type of submission this can result in up to a 4-month (120 day) decreased review time and could be critical in moving an important animal medicine to the market sooner.

The new agreement also commits the agency to work with industry to examine longer term goals.

AHI and FDA will enter into discussions on how to more broadly extend the conditional approval process currently available only to minor species to major species applications. The Minor Use/ Minor Species Act of 2004 provided a new mechanism for the approval of animal drugs. For minor species or minor uses, a sponsor can submit an application to FDA allowing the firm to market the product while continuing to collect effectiveness data to satisfy the "substantial evidence" requirement under the FD&C Act, as long as enough data has been submitted to allow the agency to determine there is a "reasonable expectation" of efficacy before it goes on the market. Of course, the application must still meet all requirements for animal, human, and environmental safety, manufacturing quality, and be properly labeled prior to marketing. The conditional approval lasts for 5 years after which time the product is fully approved or withdrawn from the market if the sponsor fails to demonstrate substantial evidence.

AHI believes that a strong case can be made to extend this provision to certain drugs proposed for major species other than those specifically for minor use. This allows earlier marketing of important products that can be studied and thoroughly tested for effectiveness because the sponsor is adding revenue to fund such studies. The data gathered under a conditional approval will be much more robust and allow the agency to have better confidence in the safety and effectiveness of the product before it issues final approval. The advantage to FDA is that it can easily terminate the marketing of a product if the sponsor fails to complete the data commitment.

21

There is no increased risk to animal for public health since safety will be assured prior to marketing. Additionally, conditional approvals are currently in place at USDA, which regulates animal vaccines and at EPA, which regulates flea and tick products for animals. Conditional approvals could be one mechanism to address the current decline in animal drug submissions and bring much-needed new product development to the market for major species.

The other policy issue that will be discussed under the new agreement will be the issue of combination medicated feed new animal drug approvals. It is common practice in the field to combine two or more drugs in a medicated feed being given to cattle, pigs, or poultry. For the past 40-plus years FDA has required that two or more approved drugs added to an animal feed must first also be approved by the agency before they can be mixed concurrently. There is a long history of FDA requiring this and dates back to a policy first established in the 1960s that considered animal feeds containing an animal drug to be a finished drug formulation. A producer or feed manufacturer can only combine approved animal drugs in feed if an application for that combination has been approved by FDA. Therefore, an animal drug sponsor obtaining an approval for a drug to be added to animal feed is responsible for filing additional new animal drug applications providing for the concurrent mixing in the feed of the newly approved drug with other approved drugs. These are essentially administrative NADA's that simply reference the approvals of the other products but still require submission of some limited data and new labeling.

This has been an onerous requirement since it can significantly delay the ability of a sponsor to market a new product because the sponsor may not submit the other application for review and approval by FDA until the new drug is first approved. Some relief was realized in 1996 at the passage of the Animal Drug Availability Act, which lessened the requirements for the approval of these combination applications, but did not eliminate the need to submit an NADA for these combinations. Experience has shown since the ADAA that few problems can be identified by the mixing of two or more approved drugs concurrently in the feed in the way of interference with the active ingredients or with changes to animal safety or human food residues.

FDA has agreed to enter into discussion with the animal drug and animal feed industry and State regulatory authorities overseeing animal feed manufacturers over the next 3 years to determine how these requirements might be modified. This could have significant future importance with the advent of the FDA proposal to move more antimicrobials used in feed to a Veterinary Feed Directive program by allowing for veterinarians to more efficiently write VFD orders for antibiotics to be mixed into feed with other non-VFD drugs. Eliminating the requirement for combination feed approvals could pave the way for a smoother implementation of the VFD program and ensure that antimicrobials added to feed are being used for therapeutic purposes only under the order of a veterinarian.

Mr. Chairman, CVM has a rigorous, science-based approval process that provides to the American public the products necessary to protect public health by protecting animal health. Every year scientists uncover new diseases in animals, some of which potentially pose a threat to human health. As more animals are raised to feed the planet and as animals are reared closer to people, we will continue to need new medicines to protect animal and human health.

The reauthorization of ADUFA will continue to provide the agency the resources necessary to maintain and improve this approval process, provide new and innovative products to allow our pets to live longer and healthier lives and contribute to food safety by keeping food animals healthy. I urge you to move a clean ADUFA bill in a timely manner so this program can continue without interruption.

Again, thank you for holding this hearing and I would be happy to answer any questions.

The CHAIRMAN. Thank you, Dr. Carnevale.

Now, Ms. Johansson, welcome. Please proceed.

STATEMENT OF JENNIFER JOHANSSON, J.D., VICE CHAIR, GENERIC ANIMAL DRUG ALLIANCE, BEL AIR, MD

Ms. JOHANSSON. Good morning. I am Jennifer Spokes Johansson, and I serve as the vice chair of the Generic Animal Drug Alliance, or GADA.

The GADA is an independent professional trade organization that represents the interests of generic animal drug companies.

Our members are focused on the development, FDA approval, and marketing of high quality generic drugs for livestock and pets.

I would like to thank the committee for inviting me to testify today on behalf of GADA in support of the reauthorization of AGDUFA, the Animal Generic Drug User Fee Act.

Just like with human drugs, generic animal drugs provide significant benefits to the public by providing cost-effective alternatives to their pioneer drug counterparts. Lower cost generic animal drug options help contribute to the safety of the Nation's food supply, the treatment of diseases in animals that can be transmitted to humans, and the ability of pet owners to provide care to their pet family members.

However, the potential cost savings to consumers from generic animal drugs cannot be achieved without broad availability of such drugs. Therefore, it is critical that the CVM review and approval process for generic drugs is both efficient and predictable.

AGDUFA was a successful first step in achieving these goals. Prior to the implementation of AGDUFA, a single CVM review of a generic application could take longer than 2 years. In most cases, multiple review cycles are needed, so if an application required three review cycles, it could take more than 6 years for that application to receive approval.

In the time it took to get the application approved, the entire market for the generic drug could change, making it no longer cost-effective to market the drug. This created a disincentive for companies to pursue generic animal drug approvals and denied the public cost-effective generics to treat their livestock and pets.

During the time of AGDUFA, CVM eliminated the application backlog and reduced the review time goal for a single review of an application to the current 270 days. In addition, CVM implemented several process enhancements and increased communications with industry.

While user fees are a significant cost to a small industry, we believe the fees have not created too much of an impediment to pursuing generic animal drug applications. In fact, we believe user fees serve as a desired gating mechanism to ensure sponsors are serious about their intent to pursue applications to approval. Furthermore, we believe the shorter review times and predictability of the review timeline are helping contribute to the growth of our industry. This growth is evidenced by the significant increase in our GADA membership, as well as an increase in the number of application sponsors paying user fees.

AGDUFA II, as agreed upon, will continue the shortened application review times from AGDUFA. While GADA would like CVM to achieve the statutory 180-day review times, the additional fees for CVM to obtain the resources needed to reach that goal are not a viable option for the generics industry.

The animal generics industry is comprised of small companies and product markets that are much smaller than those for human drugs. Therefore, we believe it is important that the review of generic drug applications be primarily funded by congressional appropriations. For this to be achieved, appropriations must continue at a level that enables FDA to meet its public health mission, and the important public policy goal of providing generic drug options for farmers and pet owners.

Financially, we believe AGDUFA II strikes a balance between the much-needed revenue stream for CVM and the realities of a small, but growing, generics industry. However, another important industry goal for AGDUFA II was to implement additional review process enhancements that recognize high quality submissions and shorten overall time to approval.

The proposed AGDUFA II enhancements will make the approval process easier to navigate, will help generic companies better meet CVM's approval expectations, and should help reduce the number of review cycles. We expect this will enable more generic products to come to market sooner.

In conclusion, it is extremely important to the generic animal drug industry that AGDUFA be reauthorized. Without timely reauthorization of AGDUFA, we likely will return to the pre-AGDUFA days when lengthy application reviews served as a disincentive to companies pursuing generic animal drugs. Reauthorization of AGDUFA is critical to continuing to make the pursuit of generic animal drug approvals viable and to continuing to increase the number of safe and effective generic animal drugs on the market.

Thank you.

[The prepared statement of Ms. Johansson follows:]

PREPARED STATEMENT OF JENNIFER JOHANSSON, J.D.

SUMMARY

GADA is an independent professional trade organization that represents the interests of generic animal drug companies. Our members are focused on the development, FDA approval, and marketing of high quality generic drugs for livestock and pets.

Generic animal drugs provide significant benefits to the public by providing cost-effective alternatives to pioneer animal drugs, just like the benefits that human generic drugs provide to patients and payers. Lower cost generic options help increase access to much-needed therapies for animals and contribute to the safety of the Nation's food supply, the ability of pet owners to provide care to their beloved pet family members, and the treatment of diseases in animals that can be transmitted to humans. The potential cost savings to consumers with generic animal drugs cannot be achieved without broad availability of such drugs. Therefore, it is crucial that we continue to explore ways to get generic animal drugs to market by providing an efficient CVM review process for approving generic animal drugs.

AGDUFA successfully reduced ANADA review cycle times, which improved the efficiency and predictability of the generic review process. Under AGDUFA, CVM eliminated the review backlog and reduced the review time for a single review of an ANADA from 700 days or more to the current 270-day goal. In addition, CVM implemented multiple process enhancements and CVM-industry communications increased, including with the addition of quarterly CVM-industry meetings. While user fees are a significant cost to a small industry, we believe the fees have not created too much of an impediment to pursuing generic animal drug applications. In fact, we believe user fees serve as a necessary gating mechanism to ensure sponsors are serious about their intent to pursue applications to approval. Furthermore, the shorter review times and predictability of the review timeline help contribute to growth of our industry and to growing employment, including in areas of the country with fewer industries to create jobs.

AGDUFA II as agreed upon will continue the shorter ANADA review times and introduce additional important review process enhancements. The proposed legislation strikes a balance between a robust revenue stream for CVM and the realities of a small but growing generics industry. We expect this will enable more generic products to come to market sooner and create incentives for more development by generic companies, as well as more innovation by pioneer companies. Thus, reauthorization of AGDUFA is crucial to continuing to make the pursuit of generic animal drug approvals viable, to promoting a healthy generics industry, and to continuing to increase the number of generic animal drugs on the market, bringing safe and effective cost-effective drug alternatives to our Nation's farmers and pet owners.

———

GENERIC ANIMAL DRUG ALLIANCE,
BEL AIR, MD 21015,
February 25, 2013.

U.S. Senate,
Committee on Health, Education, Labor, and Pensions,
Washington, DC 20510–6300.

DEAR HONORABLE MEMBERS: Thank you for the opportunity to provide testimony to the U.S. Senate Committee on Health, Education, Labor, and Pensions on behalf of the Generic Animal Drug Alliance ("GADA") in support of reauthorization of the Animal Generic Drug User Fee Act of 2008 ("AGDUFA" and "AGDUFA II"). GADA is an independent professional trade organization that represents the interests of generic animal drug companies. Our members are focused on the development, FDA approval, and marketing of high quality generic drugs for livestock and pets. We seek to provide more options to ranchers, farmers, and pet owners for affordable medical care for animals.

GADA is the only trade organization that represents the interests of generic animal drug companies in the United States. We represent the majority of sponsors who hold investigational files for Abbreviated New Animal Drug Applications ("ANADAs") and ANADAs pending approval by FDA's Center for Veterinary Medicine ("CVM"). Our member companies also hold more than half of the currently approved ANADAs.

GENERIC ANIMAL DRUGS ARE AN IMPORTANT ALTERNATIVE TO PIONEER ANIMAL DRUGS

Generic animal drugs provide significant benefits to the public by providing cost-effective alternatives to pioneer animal drugs, just like the benefits that human generic drugs provide to patients and payers. Lower cost generic options help increase access to much-needed therapies for animals and contribute to the safety of the Nation's food supply, the ability of pet owners to provide care to their beloved pet family members, and the treatment of diseases in animals that can be transmitted to humans.

Generic animal drugs are demonstrated safe and effective and go through a rigorous CVM approval process. They must meet the same high quality standards as pioneer animal drugs and are manufactured in FDA-inspected facilities, just like human drugs. However, generic animal drug options are not nearly as prevalent as their human generic counterparts. For example, a survey conducted by one of our member companies of Animal Drugs@FDA showed that only 7 percent of CVM approved drugs for dogs and cats have a CVM approved generic equivalent.

The potential cost savings to consumers from generic animal drugs cannot be achieved without broad availability of such drugs. Human generic drugs have demonstrated the value of generic alternatives to the public; in 2011 alone, human generic drugs saved consumers and the Nation's health care system $192 billion.[1] Furthermore, greater availability of generic animal drugs means that veterinarians and consumers can make animal care decisions focused on medical reasons without having to forego treatments due to costs that are often higher than what human patients pay for drug treatment. Therefore, it is crucial that we continue to explore ways to get generic animal drugs to market by providing an efficient CVM review process for approving generic animal drugs.

AGDUFA I SUCCESSFULLY REDUCED ANADA REVIEW CYCLE TIMES

To encourage a robust generic animal drug industry that provides options for the health of livestock and pets, the ANADA approval process must be efficient and predictable. Prior to the implementation of AGDUFA, companies wishing to pursue generic animal drug applications had no certainty as to how long a single CVM review of their application would take, other than that it might take longer than 2 years. In most cases, the first review yields deficiencies and multiple review cycles are required. For each additional review the application goes to the back of the queue for another lengthy review cycle. In the time it took to get an application approved, the entire market for a generic drug could change, making it no longer cost-effective to

———

[1] Generic Pharmaceutical Association Report, "Saving $1 Trillion Over 10 Years: Generic Drug Savings in the U.S. (Fourth Annual Edition, 2012)."

market the drug and denying the public cost-effective generics to treat their livestock and pets.

An unpredictable application review timeline can prove fatal to the generic animal drug industry. Generic animal drug companies tend to be smaller and have fewer resources than their pioneer company counterparts. In the pre-AGDUFA environment, it was difficult for companies to survive and there was extreme disincentive for new companies to pursue approval of generic animal drugs.

GADA believes AGDUFA was a success in improving the efficiency and predictability of the generic review process. Since enactment of AGDUFA, CVM eliminated the review backlog and reduced the review time for a single review of an ANADA from 700 days or more to the current 270 day goal. In addition, CVM implemented multiple process enhancements and CVM-industry communications increased, including the addition of quarterly CVM-industry meetings.

The establishment of review time goals created a more predictable review timeline that allows sponsors to plan for product review, approval, and launch. This helps generic animal drug options get to market more efficiently. The shorter review times also apply to post-approval manufacturing change reviews, making it easier for manufacturers to improve and modernize their manufacturing processes. Protocol reviews under investigational files also have reduced review times, which help shorten the development time prior to seeking drug approval.

While we believe AGDUFA introduced improvements to the ANADA review process, immediately after the implementation of AGDUFA the number of ANADA submissions and reactivations significantly decreased. GADA believes this apparent decrease may be because more sponsors are pursuing ANADAs through a phased approval process and those numbers are not reflected in the number of ANADAs submitted. Also, we believe the addition of user fees created a gating mechanism to ensure that sponsors only submit ANADAs if they are serious about pursuing high quality, approvable ANADAs for products that they will bring to market.

While we also saw a significant decrease in the number of generic drugs that are drug listed with FDA, we believe this is due to sponsors "cleaning up" their drug listings so as not to list products they do not market. Furthermore, we believe sponsors reduced their redundant private labels, as maintaining multiple private labels for the same product is a common practice in the animal drug industry. Thus, the reduction in the number of listed drugs does not reflect a reduction in the number of product alternatives on the market.

Since the implementation of AGDUFA, we also have seen indications that applications are on the rise and our industry is growing. During the term of AGDUFA there was an increase in the number of investigational study submissions and in the number of generic animal drug sponsors. As the only industry association for generic animal drugs, we have seen our membership increase by 53 percent since the passage of AGDUFA, including with some new sponsors planning to develop generic animal drugs and submit ANADAs.

During the term of AGDUFA, we have also seen new companies form to pursue generic animal drugs and already-established companies in the fields of new animal drugs and human drugs enter the generic animal drug industry. Thus, while user fees are a significant cost to a small industry, we believe the fees have not created a significant impediment to pursuing generic animal drug applications. Instead, we believe the shorter review times and predictability of the review timeline help contribute to growth of our industry and to growing employment, including in areas of the country with fewer industries to create jobs.

AGDUFA II WILL CONTINUE SHORTER ANADA REVIEW TIMES AND INTRODUCE MORE REVIEW PROCESS ENHANCEMENTS

Entering into AGDUFA II negotiations, the generic animal drug industry had three primary goals: (1) keep user fee costs from increasing beyond the generic industry's ability to pay; (2) keep review times at least as good as in Year 5 of AGDUFA, and (3) implement more process enhancements to help reduce overall time to approval of drug applications.

The agreed upon AGDUFA II proposed legislation includes 5-year industry fees of $38,100,000 and strikes a balance between a robust revenue stream for CVM and the realities of a small but growing generics industry. The agreed upon increase in fees from AGDUFA I are to account for inflation and estimated reductions in congressional appropriations.

GADA recognizes that user fees are intended to supplement congressional appropriations. The generic animal drug industry is comprised of small companies and the product markets are smaller than for human drugs. Therefore, we believe it is important that the review of drug applications be primarily funded via congressional appropriations and that appropriations continue at a level that enables FDA to meet its public health mission and the important public policy goal of providing generic drug options for farmers and pet owners.

Since the number of ANADA submissions each year is less predictable than the number of marketed products and application sponsors, under AGDUFA II the application fee will contribute a smaller percentage of total revenue than in AGDUFA I. This will provide more predictability to the amount of funding collected by CVM, which benefits both CVM and industry. This will also help keep the application fee as a gating mechanism to ensure submission of high quality applications, while helping prevent the application fee from becoming too high and serving as a significant disincentive for companies to submit applications. In exchange, the product fee and sponsor fee, which are primarily paid by established sponsors with products on the market and are therefore more predictable, will contribute an increased percentage of fees to the total user fee revenue.

GADA was not concerned predominantly with reducing the review times for single review cycles because the current 270-day review goal is a marked improvement over pre-AGDUFA timelines. While GADA would like CVM to achieve the statutory 180-day review times, the industry recognizes that the additional fees for CVM to obtain the resources needed to reach such goal are not a viable option for the generics industry. Therefore, the industry believes that maintaining the existing timelines is an acceptable compromise while the industry grows and becomes further established.

An important industry goal for AGDUFA II was implementing substantial process enhancements that will reward high quality submissions. The enhancements will make the approval process easier to navigate for new and established sponsors, and will help reduce the overall time to approval, thus allowing more safe and effective generic products to reach the market sooner. For example, one enhancement allows for a second, shortened review cycle of 90 or 190 days, as opposed to 270 days, when deficiencies are not substantial.

Another enhancement, the two-phased Chemistry, Manufacturing, and Controls ("CMC") technical section process, enables sponsors to submit certain parts of their CMC section to an investigational file before the entire section is complete, thereby receiving earlier CVM feedback and avoiding deficiencies later in the review process that can delay approval. A third enhancement allows sponsors making significant post-approval changes to their application that receive non-substantial deficiencies to their supplement to implement their changes 30 days after submitting their deficiency responses, rather than waiting for another 270-day review cycle.

These and other improvements introduce efficiencies to the ANADA review process and help generic drug company sponsors better meet CVM's approval expectations. It is our hope that these enhancements, along with the current 270-day single cycle review timelines, will help reduce the number of review cycles and shorten the overall time to approval for ANADAs to get generic animal drug options to market sooner.

REAUTHORIZATION OF AGDUFA SUPPORTS A HEALTHY GENERICS INDUSTRY TO GET MORE GENERIC ANIMAL DRUGS TO THE MARKET SOONER

It is extremely important to the generic animal drug industry that AGDUFA be reauthorized. Prior to its original implementation the industry feared it would not survive, as review times dragged out and few drugs and companies made it to the end of the approval process. Furthermore, there were few incentives for new companies to pursue generic animal drugs and thus, the industry could only be sustained, and the benefits of cost-saving, high-quality generic drugs for livestock and pets realized, if the few existing companies remained.

AGDUFA has introduced shorter, predictable timelines for ANADA reviews, making it easier for companies to pursue generic animal drug applications. Furthermore, it has brought review process improvements and efficiencies. AGDUFA II will continue these shortened review timelines and bring more process enhancements that will help reduce the overall time to approval. We expect that this will enable more generic products to come to market sooner and incentivize more development by generic companies, as well as more innovation by pioneer companies. Thus, reauthorization of AGDUFA is crucial to continuing to make the pursuit of generic animal drug approvals viable, to promoting a healthy generics industry, and to continuing to increase the number of generic animal drugs on the market, bringing safe and effective cost-effective drug alternatives to our Nation's farmers and pet owners.

Sincerely,

THE GENERIC ANIMAL DRUG ALLIANCE,
Generic Animal Drug Alliance Member Companies: AgriLabs, Ltd., St. Joseph, MO; AmPharmCo, Inc., Fort Worth, TX; Aratana Therapeutics, Inc., Kansas City, MO; Argenta Limited, Metuchen, NJ; Bimeda North America, Inc., Oakbrook Terrace, IL; Ceva Animal Health, Inc., Lenexa, KS; First Priority, Inc., Elgin, IL; GDL International, St. Joseph, MO; Herschel J. Gaddy & Associates, St. Joseph, MO; Lloyd, Inc., Shenandoah, IA; Med-Pharmex, Inc., Pomona, CA; Norbrook, Inc., Lenexa, KS; Nutramax Laboratories, Inc., Edgewood, MD; Pegasus Laboratories, Inc., Pensacola, FL; Pharmgate, LLC, Ramsey, NJ; Piedmont Animal Health, Greensboro, NC; Putney, Inc., Portland, ME; Rochem International, Inc., Ronkonkoma, NY; Sparhawk Laboratories, Inc., Lenexa, KS; Teva Animal Health, a wholly owned subsidiary of Bayer HealthCare, LLC, St. Joseph, MO; Vetoquinol USA Inc., Fort Worth, TX; VetPharm, Inc., East Rochester, NY; World Gen LLC, Paramus, NJ.

The CHAIRMAN. Thank you very much, Ms. Johansson.

We will now start a 5-minute round of questions. Dr. Carnevale, I will start with you.

Again, just for the record, if ADUFA were not reauthorized, what do you think would be the impact on animal health? How would it affect ranchers, farmers, and pet owners if we did not reauthorize it by October 1?

Mr. CARNEVALE. Well, Senator, clearly FDA would have to lose a number of resources that they have now, a number of staff that they have hired on to do those reviews faster. So clearly, the review times would slip back, as Dr. Dunham had mentioned earlier, back to what they had been before.

The process will slow down even more than it is now, and it is a very rigorous review process, and we understand that we are always working to try to shorten that time. Without those resources, those times will just dramatically increase.

And as far as farmers and ranchers, there are very few drugs that are approved now. It is very difficult to get a drug through the process and when it does go through, it is very important to those farmers and ranchers. So unfortunately, this will probably decrease an incentive to develop those drugs if the process is taking longer than it does today.

The CHAIRMAN. Thank you.

Ms. Johansson, again for the record, tell me what role do generic drugs for animals play in animal health? How do they help ranchers, farmers, and pet owners?

Ms. JOHANSSON. Generic drugs give alternative to the brand drugs or the pioneer drugs that are equivalent. They are equivalent in safety and effectiveness and quality, but they are lower cost options. So this provides a cost benefit for farmers, for pet owners, for ranchers. And often may enable a treatment that a pet owner or a rancher could not afford in the first place.

The CHAIRMAN. The same question I asked of Dr. Carnevale— what would be the effect if AGDUFA were not reauthorized? What would be the impact on ranchers, farmers, and pet owners if it were not reauthorized in time?

Ms. JOHANSSON. Right. As Dr. Carnevale mentioned, FDA would have to reduce their staffing and then they would not be able to review the applications in a timely manner. This would mean that less options, whether it be pioneer drugs or generic drugs, would be available to ranchers, farmers, and pet owners.

In the generics industry, we just had our first AGDFUA legislation 5 years ago. So just 5 years ago, we really were in that world where it was taking 700 days or more for a review. And it was not incentivizing companies to pursue those generic drug options.

The CHAIRMAN. Thank you both very much.

I will yield to Senator Alexander.

Senator ALEXANDER. Mr. Carnevale, give us a little historical perspective on the importance of animal health to human health. My memory of history is that, throughout world history and in our country, many epidemics have been spread by unhealthy animals. In the early days of, what, North America, the arrival of the Europeans with animals kind of led to small pox. It wiped out whole populations. Is that where all of this begins, this concern about the relationship of healthy animals to healthy people?

Mr. CARNEVALE. Yes, well fortunately, we don't have outbreaks like small pox any longer, but clearly, there is a nexus between animal and human health. Diseases are spread, as we all know, between animals and humans. And the fact is, the healthier that we can keep our animals, the healthier we can keep humans, particularly with the food supply.

It has been shown that animals that are not healthy that might go to slaughter with some clinical disease, the meat from those animals may be more tainted with bacteria than those animals that are kept healthy.

There is a long history of maintaining that animal health through vaccines. Vaccines are very important as well as animal drugs. Both of those go hand in hand to keep our food animals healthy, so that they don't spread those diseases to humans.

Of course, there have been other measures besides the use of technologies. There has been the way we have raised animals with good biosecurity techniques to keep them from being infected by pathogenic organisms that could transfer to humans. But the whole arena of agriculture, including the use of the technologies we are talking about here, has improved to maintain that separation of animal disease from human disease.

Senator ALEXANDER. We don't have to go back very far to find the time, maybe it was the 1930's, that say when there were almost no, well, there wasn't the pharmaceutical industry really. There were almost no drugs for human health. How far back do we have to go to find the development of drugs for animal health?

Mr. CARNEVALE. I would say probably in the 1950s is when we really——

Senator ALEXANDER. Not before then?

Mr. CARNEVALE. Probably not before then, I mean, I think there were probably remedies out there. There was no organized drug business, but I think probably in the 1950s, antibiotics started to become used in animals, and so, it is a fairly new industry.

Senator ALEXANDER. Ms. Johansson, you mentioned the 270-day timeline, and it sounded like what you were saying was that it was too expensive to aim for 180-day timeline, to try to take that 700 day period and get it down to 180. Is that right? That would just cost too much in user fees to do that, was that the consensus?

Ms. JOHANSSON. Well, to take the 270-day time period.

Senator ALEXANDER. Yes.

Ms. JOHANSSON. And bring it down to 180 days.

Senator ALEXANDER. Yes.

Ms. JOHANSSON. Right, would cost too much in user fees.

Senator ALEXANDER. Yes. Thank you, Mr. Chairman.

The CHAIRMAN. Thank you, Senator Alexander.

Senator Roberts.

Senator ROBERTS. Thank you, Mr. Chairman. I have a very general question, and the answer to it is yes, if I can find it here.

Dr. Carnevale, I have been getting feedback, all of us who are privileged to represent agriculture States and the animal drug community, that while there may be some minor tweaks or changes to the user fee programs that various folks would recommend generally, that my impression is that you support a clean bill, and we have a clean bill. And as the Chairman indicated, we hope that we can be successful on the Senate floor, and that we would have your support. Is that correct?

Mr. CARNEVALE. That's correct, Senator.

Senator ROBERTS. All right. Let me veer off into another concern that I have that also involves a thank you to you and all of the veterinary associations from all of our States.

As a former member of the Intelligence Committee and I was chairman for a while, I was always worried about a possible attack on our food supply, and obviously, that deals with the animal industry. And we had several exercises and in one, I was privileged—if that is the proper word for it—to play the role of the president. I emphasize that there wasn't anybody else in town, so they had to get somebody, but I think it was because of my experience on the agriculture committee and on the intelligence committee.

We went under attack—this was an exercise—and there have been numerous exercises like this. Following those exercises, and I won't go into any detail, but some very difficult, we went through what would happen in regards to an attack like hoof and mouth, and what would happen to the animal industry, and it was pretty bad.

That was some years ago. I think we have a much better understanding of that. That threat still exists. It could be easy to do by any terrorist group, but the veterinarians in Kansas, at least, and this comes down to county level, have done an excellent job of doing training to be first responders if anything like that would happen. And they know the criteria that they are supposed to follow and they have repeatedly gone to meetings statewide and even national meetings on this subject.

I just want to thank your Center for what you have been doing, and I hope you have been doing in regards to any possible threat to our food supply. And the fact that one of the first responders is your local veterinarian, who also, by the way, has a lot of trust wherever that person may be practicing.

Do you have any comment?

Mr. CARNEVALE. No. Thank you for that. I think our industry has been very forward-looking in trying to provide the vaccines that are needed for those kinds of threats and I know that is at the top of their mind.

Ever since 9/11, as you said, we have been going through those exercises. And I would only say that we are very fortunate in this country to have as safe a food supply as we do, and I think people take it for granted because those threats, as well as common threats from bacteria and viruses that do not come from terrorism, are also a threat to the food supply. And I think the farmers, the ranchers, the veterinarians, the animal drug industry all do a marvelous job of keeping our food supply safe.

But those threats are there and you are right. We have been very lucky, but I think we have also prepared very well, and I think our industry has helped with those preparations in trying to make sure the vaccines for those viral diseases that could come from terrorism are out there and ready to be used if necessary. So thank you for that, Senator.

Senator ROBERTS. I appreciate that.

Thank you, Mr. Chairman.

The CHAIRMAN. Thank you very much, Senator Roberts.

Thank you all very much. Thank you, Dr. Carnevale. Thank you, Ms. Johansson for your involvement in this effort. Hopefully, as you have heard from all of us and we have heard from you, we hope to keep this a clean bill and get it moved expeditiously through the Senate, and hopefully the same thing will happen on the House side. Thank you all very much.

The record will remain open for 10 days for further submissions by other Senators.

The CHAIRMAN. And with that, the committee will stand adjourned.

Thank you.

[Whereupon, at 10:58 a.m., the hearing was adjourned.]

○